Colin Powell

Straight to the Top

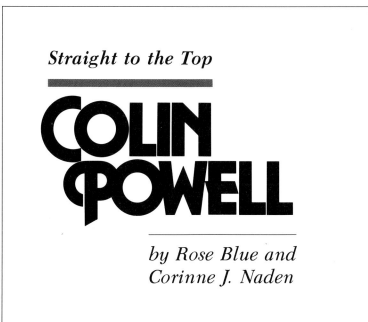

COLIN POWELL

*by Rose Blue and
Corinne J. Naden*

*The Millbrook Press
Brookfield, Connecticut
A Gateway Biography*

Library of Congress Cataloging-in-Publication Data

Blue, Rose.
Colin Powell : straight to the top / by Rose Blue and
Corinne J. Naden.
  p.   cm.
Includes index.
"A Gateway biography."
Summary: Describes the life and career of the first black chairman
of the Joint Chiefs of Staff.
ISBN 1-56294-052-X
1. Powell, Colin L.—Juvenile literature.   2. Generals—United
States—Biography—Juvenile literature.   3. United States. Army—
Biography—Juvenile literature.   4. Afro-American generals—
Biography—Juvenile literature. [1. Powell, Colin L.   2. Generals.
3. Afro-Americans—Biography.]   I. Naden, Corinne J.   II. Title.
E840.5.P68B57 1991
355'.0092—dc20   91-19121   CIP   AC
[B]

Cover photograph of Colin Powell courtesy of
Gamma-Liaison; camouflage courtesy of Ginger Giles.

Photographs courtesy of: Department of Defense: pp.
6, 27 (both), 35, 38; Wide World Photos, Inc.: pp.
9, 20 (both), 41 (both), 42; Marilyn Powell Berns:
pp. 13, 14; Conrad Waldinger: p. 17; Library of
Congress: p. 24 (top); UPI/Bettmann: p. 24 (bottom,
both); Black Star, © Dennis Brack: p. 31.

*From Rose: Dedicated to Dr. James Bell,
who is dedicated to the children,
one of those who "paved the way."*

*From Corinne: To my cousins Mary Lou
and Artie Wiesner, with love.*

*The authors thank Robert De Marshe
for his guidance through the maze of
Bronx streets and for his patience in
finding landmarks that pertained to
General Powell. Our thanks also to
Mitchell Strear for the ROTC photo
and for his help.*

U.S. troops arrive in Saudi Arabia in 1990, before the outbreak of the Persian Gulf War. They were sent after Iraq invaded the oil-rich country of Kuwait.

On *August 2, 1990,* Iraq invaded and conquered Kuwait. The news shocked the world. Kuwait is on the Persian Gulf, sandwiched between Iraq to the north and west and Saudi Arabia to the south. This is part of the troubled area called the Middle East.

Oil-rich Kuwait is a tiny desert land that is only a little larger than the state of Connecticut. Overpowered by Iraq, Kuwait asked the United Nations (U.N.) for help. Saudi Arabia, afraid of being invaded next, also turned to the world organization. The United Nations said Iraq was wrong. To protect Saudi Arabia, President George Bush sent U.S. troops there. This was the start of Operation Desert Shield. The U.S. forces were soon joined by troops from Britain, France, Egypt, and other U.N. members.

During the next few months, many countries urged Iraq to leave Kuwait. Iraq's leader, Saddam Hussein, refused. Finally, the United Nations ordered Iraq to get out of Kuwait by January 15, 1991. War was threatened.

January 15 came and went. Iraq did not budge.

One day later, on January 16, Operation Desert Shield turned into Operation Desert Storm. The United States and its allies went to war against Iraq. U.S. Secretary of Defense Richard Cheney told the nation, "The liberation of Kuwait has begun."

The war became known as the Persian Gulf War. The allied forces numbered more than half a million. Most were U.S. troops. They faced an even larger Iraqi army. The Americans were fighting a war in a desert thousands of miles from home.

Even before the first shot was fired, President Bush counted on the help of his top military adviser, the chairman of the Joint Chiefs of Staff (JCS). The JCS includes the top people in all the branches of the U.S. military. The chairman that President Bush counted on was a four-star general in the U.S. Army. His name is Colin Luther Powell.

As chairman of the JCS, Colin Powell was the highest-ranking military officer in the United States and the world's most powerful soldier. He was fifty-two years old when he took over as chairman on October 1, 1989. That made him the youngest chairman ever. He was also the first black American to have this job.

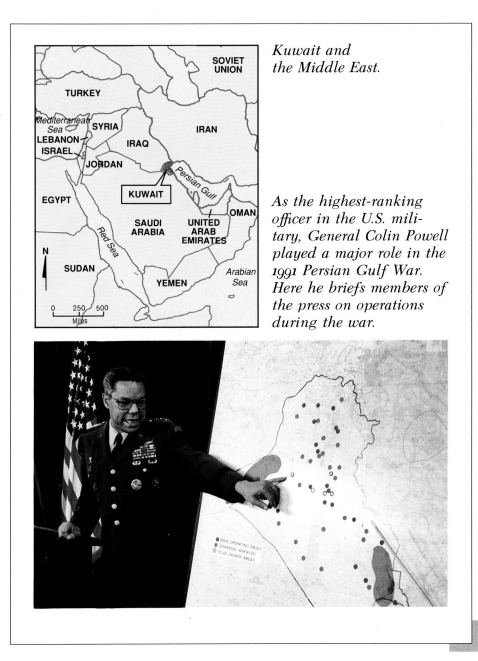

Kuwait and the Middle East.

As the highest-ranking officer in the U.S. military, General Colin Powell played a major role in the 1991 Persian Gulf War. Here he briefs members of the press on operations during the war.

Colin Luther Powell is an impressive person. He stands six feet, one inch tall and weighs two hundred pounds. His dark, close-cropped hair is graying. It is said (although probably not to his face) that he has "teddy bear" good looks. His husky frame is held straight. He *looks* like a general.

Powell is every inch the military professional. He is quiet, serious, and businesslike. His manner is polished and even-tempered. He also has a sense of humor, and he can talk to civilians and military people with the same ease.

Powell was born into a poor black immigrant family. How did he rise to become the country's top military man? There was no magic shortcut. Powell once said, "People keep asking the secret of my success. There isn't any secret. I work hard and spend long hours. It's as simple as that." He advised young people, "There is no substitute for hard work and study. Nothing comes easy."

Things *were not easy* for young Colin Powell. He was born in Harlem in New York City on April 5, 1937. Many blacks and other minorities live in Harlem. It is part of the borough of Manhattan. New York City, the nation's largest city, has four other boroughs—Brooklyn, Queens, Staten Island, and the Bronx. When Colin was still a young child, his family moved to the South Bronx. He grew up in a four-bedroom apartment on Kelly Street.

The South Bronx was, and still is, a poor neighborhood. Colin's mother and father came to America in the 1920s from the island of Jamaica in the Caribbean. Both parents worked in the garment district of New York City. Maud, Colin's mother, was a seamstress. Luther, his father, was a shipping clerk.

Colin Powell grew up to be a serious, strong military leader. But tears can still cloud his eyes when he speaks of his mother and father. They both died in the 1980s. "As I grow older," he has said, "I have greater and greater affection for my parents."

Maud and Luther Powell were serious people with a dream. They wanted a better life for Colin and his sister, Marilyn, who is five and a half years older than Colin. For the Powells, education was the key to a better life. Colin's mother graduated from high school; his father did not. If Maud Powell got annoyed at her husband, she would remind him just *who* had the high school diploma.

The Powells taught their children that success comes with hard work. "You must set a goal and do your job well," they said.

A reporter once suggested that Colin Powell got to the top because his parents taught him values. The general had this reply: "Kids don't pick up training because parents sit around and talk to them about values. Children watch their parents *live* values. Youngsters don't care what you say, but they watch what you do."

The future general grew up in a warm, loving, hardworking family. His sister, Marilyn, remembers that when the family first moved to the South Bronx, there were few children his age in the neighborhood. So Colin went everywhere with her. "He was a tagalong brother," she says. She recalls that he was "really a pretty average boy," but he always "had a sense of direction." She was not surprised by his later success, only by the "greatness of it." Today Marilyn Powell Berns is married and is a teacher in Santa Ana, California.

Colin grew up in a warm, close-knit family. Here he is shown at about age seven, with his mother and his sister, Marilyn.

Colin, age eight, and Marilyn, age fourteen.

The neighborhood around Kelly Street included people of many kinds. There were blacks and Puerto Ricans, and there was a large Jewish population. As Colin grew older, he played stickball on the streets with friends. He served as an altar boy at St. Margaret's Episcopal Church. And, of course, he went to school—first to the neighborhood elementary school, and then to Morris High School nearby. After school, he worked at a furniture store in his neighborhood. He learned a little of the Yiddish language from the store's Jewish owners. "I had a great childhood," he later recalled.

Colin was not an honor student. He admits that at school he sometimes "horsed around." His sister laughingly says that he was a "late bloomer." A late bloomer is someone who succeeds in school or at a career at an older age than most other people do. Colin Powell gives hope to all late bloomers who are C students. That was his grade average during high school and college.

Powell went to City College of New York (CCNY) in 1954. The school is now part of City University of New York (CUNY). He had no career in mind, but City College was free to New York students. He worked part-time after classes.

In his second semester of college, Powell joined the Reserve Officers Training Corps (ROTC). This program trains college students to become officers in the army. Powell's group was known as the Pershing Rifles. He later said that he joined because he liked the uniform. Actually, the military had always impressed him. He was a young boy during World War II and a teenager during the Korean War.

According to an old saying, some people "find a home in the army." In other words, sometimes a person is just right for military life. Colin Powell and the army seemed just right together. This C student got straight A's in his ROTC classes in all four years of college. When his group took summer training at Fort Bragg, North Carolina, he was named "outstanding cadet."

Powell earned a degree in geology (the study of the history of the earth, especially through rocks) from CCNY in 1958. He graduated at the top of his ROTC group. He was a Pershing Rifles company commander, a cadet colonel (ROTC's highest

*Powell's Reserve Officers Training Corps
(ROTC) unit, the Pershing Rifles, posed for
this picture in 1958. Powell is in the top row,
fifth from the left. He was a cadet colonel,
the highest rank in the ROTC.*

rank), and a "distinguished military graduate." The late bloomer was blooming.

One of Powell's ROTC classmates at CCNY was Mitchell Strear, who later became a school principal in New York City. Strear recalls: "Even back then Colin drew attention when he entered a room. At the age of eighteen, his bearing, manner, and presence were special. You just knew he would become a leader. The infantry has a motto: 'Follow me.' Colin's manner of acceptance of responsibility and leadership all said 'Follow me.'"

Powell decided to follow the army. On June 9, 1958, he became a second lieutenant. He earned sixty dollars a week. His parents encouraged him. They felt that, like most young men at the time, he would have been drafted into the military anyway. The Powells thought that their son would serve a tour of duty, then come home and get a "real job." Instead, he went into the army to stay. He had "found a home." To him, a career in the military was "an honorable profession and a contribution to society."

But success in the military was not certain for Powell. In his profession, the most successful people have usually come from "the Point"—the U.S. Military Academy at West Point, New York. Many famous American generals were West Pointers. They include President Dwight D. Eisenhower and General Douglas MacArthur, who fought in World War II, and Robert E. Lee and Ulysses S. Grant, both generals in the Civil War.

General Colin Powell did not go to West Point. Yet he did make it to the top in the army. He once said: "Although I had to compete in my military schooling with West Pointers . . . my CCNY foundation was so solid, I never regretted going anywhere but to City."

Lieutenant Powell was sent to training school at Fort Benning, Georgia. At that time, blacks and whites were segregated—kept apart by law—in many places. In the South, blacks were required to attend separate schools, which were generally not as good as the schools for whites. Blacks ate at segregated restaurants, sat in separate seats on buses and in movie theaters, and drank from separate water fountains.

In the 1950s, segregation was widespread in the South. Top: A sign points to a railway waiting room for blacks in Mississippi. Bottom: Soldiers block black students from an all-white high school in Little Rock, Arkansas, in 1957.

Late in the 1950s, that was beginning to change. Blacks all over the country were beginning to demand, and win, civil rights—the basic rights of all citizens. But many whites still wanted the races to be kept separate. Thus, when Colin Powell went to Fort Benning at the age of twenty-one, he felt the shock of racism for the first time.

"On Kelly Street in the South Bronx, everybody was a minority," Powell later said. "I didn't know what a 'majority' was." But he realized his status soon enough. When he stopped at a restaurant in Columbus, Georgia, the waitress refused to serve him a hamburger unless he went around to the back door.

Even after he became the army's top man, Powell never forgot how much blacks had suffered. He became a student of black history and an admirer of Martin Luther King, Jr., who led the civil rights struggle in the 1950s and 1960s. Powell has advised young black Americans: "Don't let your blackness, your minority status, be a problem to you. Let it be a problem to somebody else. . . . Beat them at it. Prove they're wrong. If you work hard, do the best you can, take advantage of every opportunity that's put in front of you, success will come your way."

In his own career, Powell has done just that. "In the army," he once said, "I never felt I was looked down on by my white colleagues. I've been given the opportunity to compete fair and square with them." It helped, he added, that he "came along at a time of change, a time of growth in civil rights."

Today, blacks make up about twelve percent of the U.S. population but about thirty percent of the U.S. Army. Why? The main reason is opportunity. Segregation is against the law, but blacks still face many barriers to success. The military offers a chance for education and advancement. It also offers less racism than probably any other career.

Black Americans have fought with honor in all of America's wars. But the military has not always treated them so honorably. Blacks fought in the American Revolution, but many were slaves. During the War of 1812 against the British, blacks fought in the Battle of New Orleans. But General Andrew Jackson had to argue with the government before they were paid.

Black troops fought in the Civil War, in World

War I, and in World War II. They served bravely and well. But they were segregated—in separate fighting units, separate officers' clubs, and separate jobs. Men who cooked or served food to officers, for instance, were nearly always black.

In 1948, after World War II, President Harry S. Truman signed Executive Order 9981. It *officially* ended segregation in the armed forces. The problem didn't go away overnight. There was still racism. But today there is no segregation in any of the U.S. armed services.

Besides Colin Powell, a number of blacks have had outstanding military careers. During World War II, Benjamin O. Davis, Sr., became the first black general in the U.S. Army. Benjamin O. Davis, Jr., his son, became a lieutenant general in the U.S. Air Force and the highest-ranking black in the military in 1965. At West Point in 1932, his classmates had refused to talk to him because of his race.

Black women have also succeeded in the military. Such people have made Colin Powell's path easier. "We should be grateful," he once said, "for what all these men and women have done before. We cannot let the torch drop."

Blacks have a long history in the U.S. military. Top:
A black regiment leads an attack during the Civil War.
Left: World War II general Benjamin O. Davis, Sr.
Right: Benjamin O. Davis, Jr., as an Air Force pilot.

After completing his training in 1958, Second Lieutenant Powell spent his first tour of duty in West Germany. As a platoon leader, he was in charge of forty men. His advice for all second lieutenants is: "Just take care of your soldiers. Too many young officers say, 'Gee, one of these days I'm going to be the chairman [of the JCS] or the chief of staff or I'm going to be a general.' I tell 'em, 'Oh, stop all that. Just go do the best you can and stop worrying about it.' "

Powell's second duty station was Fort Devens, Massachusetts. The year was 1960. By then he was a twenty-three-year-old first lieutenant. The army kept him busy, but he found time for racketball, and for a blind date. She was Alma Vivian Johnson, the daughter of a high school principal from Birmingham, Alabama. She had a degree in audiology and taught students who were hearing impaired. Colin and Alma were married on August 25, 1962.

Early in the 1960s, the United States was sending military advisers to help the government of South Vietnam fight a Communist rebellion. It was the beginning of the Vietnam War. Powell, now a captain, spent 1963 as an adviser to a South Vietnamese infantry battalion. While he was there, he stepped in a trap that pierced his foot. He was out of action for a few weeks, and he won the Purple Heart. Later that year he was awarded the Bronze Star. By 1991 the general wore twenty-one decorations, six of them for combat.

The Powell's first child, Michael, was born while his father was in Vietnam. A daughter, Linda, was born in 1965, and a second daughter, Annemarie, was born about five years later.

When he came home from Vietnam, Powell was sent to the Army Command and General Staff College at Fort Leavenworth, Kansas. He asked an officer there about going to graduate school. "Your college grades aren't good enough," the officer said. He seemed to mean that Powell wasn't smart enough. That made Powell angry—and determined. When his Leavenworth class graduated, he was number 2 out of 1,244. How did he do it? Simple, the general later recalled: "Hard work."

In 1968, Powell was a major, and he was back in Vietnam. A helicopter in which he was flying crashed and burned. Powell was thrown clear, but

Soldiers emerge from a helicopter on a hilltop in Vietnam during the war there. Colin Powell served two tours of duty in Vietnam.

A Purple Heart, one of six combat decorations that Colin Powell earned during his career.

he ran back and pulled everyone to safety. For his bravery, he was awarded the Soldier's Medal and another Bronze Star.

When he was back home again, Powell entered graduate school in Washington, D.C. He earned a master's degree in business administration from George Washington University in 1971.

Getting to the top in the military is a lot like getting to the top in any business. It doesn't hurt if the boss or the president knows your name. It doesn't hurt if people get to know how good you are. Powell's next move put him alongside some important people in the U.S. government. At the age of thirty-five, in 1972, he was one of seventeen military people picked to be special government assistants. They are called White House Fellows.

He served in the Office of Management and Budget. The deputy director of this office, Frank C. Carlucci, was very impressed with Major Powell. The director, Caspar W. Weinberger, was also impressed. They both admired Powell's quiet efficiency and his competence. The three men became friends. This was important to Powell's future career.

But in 1973 it was time for overseas duty again. Now a lieutenant colonel, Powell took command of the First Battalion, 32nd Infantry, in Korea. It was a unit torn by trouble. Blacks and whites didn't get along. Drug use was common. Powell later said that he "threw the bums out of the army and put the drug users in jail." But that wasn't all he did. After a few months, blacks and whites in the unit were working and living together without trouble. This experience made Powell deeply concerned about drug abuse, especially among young people.

After Korea, Powell began a chain of jobs that put him on a path straight to the top. He worked at the Defense Department, in Washington, D.C. He attended the National War College for advanced military schooling. He went to Fort Campbell, Kentucky, to command the Second Brigade, 101st Airborne Division. Then he returned to Washington, to work at the Defense Department and the Department of Energy.

His next posts were Fort Carson, Colorado, and Leavenworth, Kansas, where he commanded some

18,000 soldiers. He rose higher and higher in the military chain of command. He was promoted to colonel, to brigadier general, and then to major general. By 1982 he wore two stars.

All this moving from place to place was hard for the Powells and their three children. Like many military families, they were very close. Friends say that the general is extremely devoted to his wife and children. Powell spent as much time with his family as he could. He also tried to find time for his favorite hobby—fixing up old cars.

In 1983, Powell was called back to Washington once again. His old friends, Frank Carlucci and Caspar Weinberger, remembered him. He became the top military aide, first to Carlucci, who was now deputy secretary of defense, and then to Weinberger, secretary of defense in President Ronald Reagan's administration.

Weinberger came to depend more and more on his military aide. He admired the quiet, competent way in which General Powell ran the day-to-day workings of the giant Defense Department. Powell was able to get along with all kinds of people and to keep them all working together.

The Powell family in 1987.
From the left are Annemarie, Michael,
Linda, and Colin and Alma Powell.

It wasn't easy. The United States had some bumpy times during those years. In 1983, U.S. troops invaded the Caribbean island of Grenada to restore order there. And 241 U.S. Marines were killed in a terrorist attack in Lebanon.

Powell's work during this time brought him power and influence in the U.S. government. He earned a third star, becoming a lieutenant general. He also earned a job he had long wanted.

In the middle of 1986, Powell took over the U.S. Army Fifth Corps, headquartered in Frankfurt, then West Germany. This was his longtime dream of an infantry command. While he was in charge of this 75,000-member corps, he said he was "probably the happiest general in the world."

If so, it didn't last long. By the end of the year, Frank Carlucci was on the phone from Washington. The Reagan administration was in trouble over what became known as the Iran-contra scandal. Members of the administration were accused of selling weapons to Iran, ignoring a ban on such sales. They were also charged with supplying arms to rebels in Nicaragua. Congress had forbidden such action.

Carlucci wanted Powell to return to Washington and become the new national security adviser to President Reagan. The administration needed someone to help straighten things out.

The general politely said no. He had the job he wanted. He had earned it. He didn't want to leave.

Carlucci called twice more. Powell still said no. Then Carlucci told him, "The commander in chief needs you." By "commander in chief," he meant the president.

How could the general refuse? The next day President Ronald Reagan himself called. He said that he knew Powell wanted to stay in Germany. But, the president added, "We need you here."

The good soldier returned to the United States. Shortly after his return, he and his wife received tragic news. Their son, Michael, an army lieutenant in Germany, had been in a jeep accident. At first, doctors said he wouldn't live. Then they said he wouldn't walk. But he did both. It was a long recovery, but in time Michael was able to enter Georgetown University Law School in Washington, D.C. He married his college sweetheart, and they have the Powells' first grandchild, a boy named Jeffrey.

General and Mrs. Powell's older daughter, Linda, became an actress in New York City. The youngest, Annemarie, followed in her brother's and sister's footsteps and attended William and Mary College in Virginia.

Once back in the United States, the Powells were reunited with their children, and the general's career continued to rise. As national security adviser, Powell proved to be the right man for the job. From December 1987 until January 1989, he kept things running smoothly between the White House and government agencies. He supervised important summit meetings between President Reagan and the leader of the Soviet Union, Mikhail Gorbachev.

No matter how big his job, the general always seemed to have time for people. At a White House dinner during Powell's last days as national security adviser, a black waiter said to him, "I know you're leaving. I just wanted to thank you and say that it's been good to see you here. I was in World War II, and I fought all the way from North Africa to Italy."

Powell replied, "Brother, I ought to be thanking you."

As national security adviser to President Ronald Reagan, Powell held an important job. Here he meets in the White House with (from left) Deputy Secretary of Defense Frank Carlucci, Secretary of State George Shultz, and President Reagan.

George Bush became president in January 1989. One of the first things he did was to put the general out of a job. Bush told Powell that he wanted to name his own national security adviser. This is a common practice, and Powell understood. But even so, he began to wonder if the time had come to leave the army.

He talked it over with his family and close friends. Then, in his organized, precise way, he made up two lists: "Reasons to Leave the Army" and "Reasons to Stay in the Army." The "Leave" list had only one item: He could make about $1 million yearly just for giving lectures. The "Stay" list had many items. The most important one was simply that Colin Powell loved the army.

Powell stayed. He earned a fourth star, becoming a full general. Not many soldiers wear four stars in the U.S. Army. That is the top; ordinarily, you can't go higher. However, Congress can, and sometimes does, create the rank of five-star general. World War II heroes Dwight Eisenhower and Omar Bradley wore five stars.

Powell also got a new job in April 1989. He took

over the U.S. Forces Command, at Fort McPherson, Georgia. To say that this was a big job is a big understatement. He was in command of all troops stationed in the United States. That included some 250,000 active soldiers and 300,000 in the reserve and National Guard. His budget was $10 billion.

Big job or no, bigger things were coming. Later that year, President Bush named Powell as the first black chairman of the Joint Chiefs of Staff (JCS).

The Joint Chiefs of Staff is an agency in the Department of Defense. It advises the president on military policy. The JCS has six members: the chairman, the vice chairman, the chiefs of staff of the army and the air force, the chief of naval operations, and the commandant of the Marine Corps. The group meets in Washington, D.C., three times a week, in a windowless room called "the tank." These six people decide on U.S. military matters. There are more than two million Americans in military service. Being chairman of the JCS is a big, and mostly top-secret, job.

The Powells moved to an elegant old house that is reserved for the chairman of the Joint Chiefs. It stands on a hill in Fort Myers, Virginia, a suburb of

Powell is sworn in as chairman of the Joint Chiefs of Staff on October 3, 1989. Secretary of Defense Dick Cheney administers the oath of office; Alma Powell is shown holding the Bible.

the nation's capital. The house has a grand view across the Potomac River. But the general joked that he sometimes longed for an army base, so that he could enjoy his hobby of fixing up old cars. Having old cars around the yard in Fort Myers, he said with a grin, "drags down the neighborhood."

As chairman of the Joint Chiefs, Powell had to handle a crisis almost immediately. On December 20, 1989, some 26,000 U.S. troops invaded the Central American country of Panama. They ousted Panama's dictator, Manuel Noriega, who was wanted in the United States on drug trafficking charges.

The biggest challenge was yet to come, however. More than anyone else, General Powell is given credit for the U.S. military success after Iraq refused to leave Kuwait in 1990–1991. The American military forces performed almost perfectly. From the start of the Persian Gulf War on January 16, allied planes bombed military and government facilities in Iraq. They were so accurate and thorough that when the ground war began, on February 24, Iraq surrendered in just one hundred hours.

The Persian Gulf War ended in a cease-fire on

February 28, 1991. It had lasted forty-three days. The United States and its allies had very few casualties. American men and women, weapons, and machines did such a good job that a wave of patriotism flooded the United States. Yellow ribbons (which stood for the hope that the troops would return safely) and American flags were everywhere, flying from houses, offices, and trees.

President Bush talked to Congress and the American people on March 6, 1991. "The war is over," he said. He gave credit for the battle plan and the smooth operation of the war to Colin Powell and to General H. Norman Schwarzkopf, who commanded the allied troops. There was even some talk of five stars for both men.

Obviously, George Bush was pleased with his choice for chairman of the Joint Chiefs of Staff. At the time Bush had named him, there were several men who had been generals longer than Powell had. Even so, no one had been really surprised at the president's choice. And, if anyone objected, no one had objected out loud. Instead, a Washington politician had said of the general: "I can't think of anyone who is critical of him."

Left: Tanks belonging to the 82nd Airborne Division move across the desert in Saudi Arabia. U.S. forces performed almost perfectly during the Persian Gulf War, and much of the credit went to Powell. Below: Powell visited the troops in Saudi Arabia in December 1990, just before fighting broke out. Here he uses a soldier's head as a "writing desk" to sign an autograph.

The success of U.S. forces in the Persian Gulf War made Powell a national hero. A few weeks after the victory, he visited his former high school in the Bronx and spoke to students there.

After the Persian Gulf War, there were many rumors about what Powell would do next. Would he leave the army? Would he enter politics?

From what people say of him, General Powell probably can do anything he wants. He almost sounds too good to be true. But he *is* true, say those who know him. What you see is really what you get.

President George Bush says: "It is most important that the general of the Joint Chiefs of Staff be a person of breadth, judgment, experience, and total integrity. Colin Powell has all these qualities and more."

Perhaps the most glowing words come from former Secretary of Defense Caspar Weinberger: "He is one of the very best persons I have ever worked with in any of the positions I've had." Weinberger also says: "He is a superb soldier. . . . He is a great patriot in the best and truest sense of the word. . . . He is a born leader. . . . He is a man of high moral standards."

It is hard to top such praise. But former Deputy Defense Secretary Graham Claytor has an idea concerning General Powell's future: "Colin would make a great president of the United States."

Important Dates

<hr>

1937	April 5: Colin Luther Powell is born in Harlem, New York City.
1954	Graduates from Morris High School, Bronx, New York. Enters City College of New York.
1955	Joins ROTC unit at CCNY.
1958	Graduates from CCNY with a degree in geology. Commissioned second lieutenant in U.S. Army. Goes to Georgia for basic training. Sent on first tour of duty, in West Germany.
1960	Becomes first lieutenant. Sent to second duty station, Fort Devens, Massachusetts.
1962	August 25: Marries Alma Vivian Johnson.
1963	Now a captain, Powell earns a Purple Heart in Vietnam. Son Michael is born.
1965	Daughter Linda is born.

1968	Now a major, sent on second tour of duty in Vietnam.
1971	Earns master's degree in business administration, George Washington University, Washington, D.C. Daughter Annemarie is born.
1972	Named White House Fellow.
1973	Now a lieutenant colonel. Sent on tour of duty in Korea.
1974	Serves tour of duty in Washington, D.C.
1975	Attends National War College, in Washington, D.C.
1976	Now a colonel, sent to Fort Campbell, Kentucky.
1977–1982	Holds various posts and achieves rank of major general.
1983–1986	Serves as military aide to secretary of defense. Becomes a lieutenant general.
1986	Takes command of Army Fifth Corps, Frankfurt, West Germany.
1987–1989	Serves as national security adviser, Reagan administration.
1989	April 4: Earns four stars. October 1: Named chairman of Joint Chiefs of Staff.
1990–1991	Oversees successful operation of Persian Gulf War.

Index